D1571266

discouragement: REASONS AND ANSWERS

"Hear my cry, O God;
listen to my prayer.
From the ends of the earth
I call to you, I call as my heart grows faint;
lead me to the rock that
is higher than I."

Psalm 61:1–2

Discouragement:
reasons *and* answers

K.P. Yohannan

BOOKS

a division of Gospel for Asia

www.gfa.org

ISBN 978-1-59589-064-1

Published by gfa books, a division of Gospel for Asia
1800 Golden Trail Court, Carrollton, TX 75010 USA
phone: (972) 300-7777
fax: (972) 300-7778
Printed in the United States of America

For information about other materials, visit our website:
www.gfa.org

10 11 12 13 14 15 / 5 4 3 2 1

Table of Contents

Introduction

———•◦•———

When things go well, our spirits soar high, and we are filled with hope and optimism.

But when we scrape the bottom in discouragement, we feel disillusioned and exposed. We usually hide the hurt from others beneath a public image of superficiality and a religious cliché or two. Yet deep on the inside, we struggle to maintain hope for the rough winds that jerk our sails, and we are afraid of what is to come.

The Apostle Paul had to deal with such times. He said, "We despaired even of life" (2 Corinthians 1:8). While in light of achieving great things for God, he fell into the depth of sudden despair. Lonely, weary and emotionally drained, this powerful strong Christian leader hit the bottom. And such low times are definitely not limited to someone like this saint of old.

But discouragement is not unbeatable. In fact, God's Word is filled with encouragement for us. It is important that we cling to these words when we feel crushed by what we are going through.

My prayer is that this booklet will point you toward these places of hope. May it help you to look up when your heart is heavy and to see Christ, our only answer.

CHAPTER ONE

Uncovering the Deceptions

———•••———

Whether we realize it or not, discouragement is one of the most powerful weapons Satan uses to hinder us and keep us from experiencing the abundant life Christ promised.

Look at what David the psalmist said: "Oh, that I had the wings of a dove! I would fly away and be at rest" (Psalm 55:6).

Here is a soul who wants to quit on life and get away from everything. Discouragement can bring us to that point. Most of us have probably felt like this at one point or another.

Discouragement is like wearing glasses with dark gray lenses; everything you see is dark and melancholy. Even though you may be surrounded by hundreds of good things, you are unable to feel joy or see any hope for your life.

Webster's Dictionary defines discouragement as "the act of discouraging . . . depression or weakening of confidence; dejection." It is also explained as "that which deters, or tends to deter, from an undertaking."[1]

In practical terms, it's the loss of courage, and sometimes discouragement goes as far as losing the courage to keep living, when nothing seems worth fighting for. The sky seems dark.

When we are discouraged, there are several things that begin to happen to us that warp our sense of reality. We remain discouraged and overtaken if we continue to believe these deceptions.

Cloud of Despair

First of all, we temporarily lose our perspective and become disoriented and confused. Our attitudes and responses are not what they should be, and we paint the night darker than it really is.

When somebody says to us, "Why are you so sad? Don't you know everything will be okay?" we reply, "How do you know what I am going through? I don't believe you."

We can find ourselves saying and feeling

things like, "Everyone is against me." True, one or two people may betray you, there may be an accident or a setback, but the truth of the matter is there are people who love you and most things are going well. When we are discouraged, however, our minds become so foggy that we cannot see things in proper perspective.

Has God Forsaken Us?

Second, we forget how God has been with us in the past. It feels like our prayers are bouncing off the ceiling, and we ask ourselves if God has forsaken us. The love and kindness we have known before seem so distant and faint. We overlook the many times we have experienced God's grace and mercy.

In addition, the ways God has used us powerfully to accomplish His purposes before are forgotten. The meaningful friendships He used and the help He provided through others are lost in our memory. We simply don't clearly see our part in His plan or who He has made us to be when we are discouraged.

The Apostle Peter was no exception. After witnessing the miraculous feeding of 5,000 people with just two fish and some loaves of bread, the disciples cast out to sea, leaving Jesus behind. Then, in the middle of the night, they saw Him walking toward them on the stormy waters.

Peter, emboldened by the sight of Jesus, asked to walk on the water as well. He got out of the boat and walked on the water all the way until they were face-to-face. Then Peter turned away and saw the wind.

He was frightened. In fact, he was so terrified that he forgot all that Jesus had just done, and he began to sink (see Matthew 14:13–33).

Likewise, we become so occupied by our immediate dilemma that we are blind to the miracles we have experienced before.

In essence, says Welsh minister Martyn Lloyd-Jones, "What accounts for most of our failures in Christian living is our failure to realize what we are. It is our failure to realize what God has done to us, what has happened to us."[2]

Problems Bigger Than Life

Third, little problems become mammoth-sized to us when we are discouraged. Tiny issues loom huge. Think about a young child blowing up a balloon until the balloon becomes so large that the child can't see anything else. It's like this when we face discouragement. We can't see anything except for the problem right in front of us.

Or think of what happens when a little pebble gets into our shoe. Even though it is a tiny thing, after a short time we are unable to think of anything else. In the same way, small irritations can seem like much larger problems when we are discouraged.

Nothing but an Empty Tank

Finally, in times of discouragement, motivation drains away and hope departs. There is an emotional breakdown. The fuel is gone, and the tank is empty. Someone says to you, "Smile," but you can't. And trying makes you feel like a phony who is pretending.

You start thinking, "Why am I studying? Why am I working?" The drive to be diligent and commit yourself vanishes. The temptation to give up becomes strong. You think, "I tried, but nobody understood. Nobody even said a kind word. Why bother anymore? I will just quit." In extreme cases, we can feel like quitting on life. It seems like we have done everything we know how to do, but nothing seems to work.

Remember that discouragement is a weapon the Enemy uses against us. Satan, the Enemy of our soul, seeks to blind us and use these adverse circumstances to keep us from what God desires for our lives.

CHAPTER TWO

The Reasons for Discouragement

------•••------

"Why are you in despair, O my soul?" (Psalm 42:5a, NASB). When we're discouraged, we can find ourselves asking this same question. Sometimes it is quite clear to us what triggered our season of discouragement. But many times the season is so cloudy, we're really not sure. We just know we can't seem to get out.

As we take the time to analyze the lives of people in Scripture who were discouraged, we will find there are reasons for discouragement that are repeated. Knowing these causes for our discouragement sometimes helps us get a handle on curing it.

Unnoticed and Unappreciated

One reason for discouragement is simply that we feel unappreciated by others. Think about the despair that must have filled the prophet Jeremiah as he wrote Lamentations. To read that book is depressing, but imagine living through it and writing it. In reality, Jeremiah's life was one continuous story of sadness. His care for the people, his love for the nation and his devotion to God were all met with hatred. Who besides God appreciated all that he did?

I heard about a man who had once lived in the slums. He was very discouraged. He would say to himself, "I don't want to try anymore. I just want to quit and go back to living the way I used to."

In the slums, he had lived a life filled with drugs and alcohol. He had committed the vilest sins imaginable, everything short of murder. He was living in the pit of hell when God rescued him, and he was born again.

Even though this man devoted his time to reading and devouring the Word of God and experienced a radically changed life, he still struggled with flashbacks of old memories. He found himself often criticized and put down by members of the local church he attended. Crying alone, he would lament that "nobody sees the distance I have covered. Nobody notices the changes God has brought about in me. Nobody cares. Nobody appreciates me."

If you are a wife, you likely have thought many times, "If only my husband understood what is involved in raising the children. If only he appreciated how much time it takes to prepare meals and keep the house clean."

If you are a husband who is godly and caring, you may have thought, "If only my wife valued all that I do at work. She never appreciates the long hours I spend supporting this family. All I hear is, 'It is not enough.' I've tried the best I know how to love her and care for the children, but it seems like nothing I do is good enough."

If you are a student, maybe you think to yourself, "If only my teachers understood where I am coming from. It seems like they can only see when I fail, but never appreciate the progress I've made."

Some may say that it isn't spiritual to worry about acknowledgment or appreciation. Whether the reason is spiritual or not, we are all human and can find ourselves discouraged by feeling unappreciated.

Misunderstood

We can also become discouraged when people misunderstand us or misread our motives. Think of Hannah, when she went to the temple to pray. In her prayers to God, Hannah wept so hard that Eli, the priest, accused her of being drunk. Imagine how that added to Hannah's discouragement about not having a child.

In Matthew, Jesus talks about how John the Baptist fasted, neither eating nor drinking, and the Pharisees of the day said he had a demon. But then Jesus came eating and drinking, and they said He was a drunkard and a glutton (see Matthew 11:18–19).

The problem is that sometimes, no matter how hard we try, we cannot convince others of our good intentions. In the end, all we do is waste our energy and our time.

As human beings, we all misunderstand each other. Like Stephen Covey says, "We see the world, not as *it is*, but as *we are*."[1]

Misunderstandings are our constant companions as we walk with Christ. A.W. Tozer says, "[The Christian life] means ostracism, misunderstanding, it means wandering lonely; it means that I carry upon me the stigma of the cross."[2]

Jesus closes the passage in Matthew with, "But wisdom is justified by her children" (Matthew 11:19, NKJV). Only the end result will show the spirit behind what we do. What people think of us in the meantime doesn't matter. However, we definitely can be tempted to be discouraged when we follow God closely, only to be misunderstood.

Dead Ends

When our hard work seems to accomplish nothing, we are prone to discouragement. "We've worked hard all night," said the disciples, "and haven't caught anything" (Luke 5:5).

We expect our labors to result in something good, but often this is not the case. Maybe a man works 10 or 12 hours a day trying to make a living and support his family, but they only get further in debt. Maybe a woman studies to pass important exams but then fails them instead. We wonder, "What is the point of all my labor?"

Think of the story of Adoniram Judson. Forsaking a comfortable life in America, he and his wife, Nancy, traveled to Burma to preach the Gospel. They worked seven long years before they saw anyone come to Christ and watched as many fellow missionaries died or went home. Every one of their children died. Adoniram was imprisoned, and finally Nancy died as well. Although they had been clearly called by God, the Judsons faced constant hardships without seeing much fruit.[3]

Remember Elijah? He fled for his life and was discouraged to the point that he "prayed

19

that he might die" (1 Kings 19:4). What discouraged Elijah was how everyone else had fallen away. He put so much effort into the ministry, but where was the result? "I am the only one left," he said (1 Kings 19:10).

Most of us have all kinds of unmet expectations. Maybe you expected to be healed by now. Perhaps you waited for the check or the telephone call to come or simply for a certain person to be kind to you. After all, you have prayed, so where are the results?

It is good to remember in these times that we don't see the end of our story yet. When Elijah had no way of knowing, God saw the 7,000 men who had not bowed their knee to Baal (see 1 Kings 19:18). God sees more than we can see, and He knows the good end to our story.

Our Own Failures

Another reason for discouragement is our introspection as we look at our failures. We look back into our own lives and see how many times we have failed, and then discouragement seeks to pull us down.

Peter looked back at all his failures and thought, "It's all over for me. I am going back to my old profession, fishing."

"But, Peter," we might say, "Why are you doing that? Aren't you the one who spoke truthfully of the deity of Christ? Jesus Himself said to you, 'And I tell you that you are Peter, and on this rock I will build my church' (Matthew 16:18). You are the one who walked on the water. You are one of the three disciples chosen to be so close to God!"

And Peter might have responded to us, "All that you said is true. But really, I am just like Judas. I used vulgar words to swear that I didn't know my Lord. I am not worthy to be His disciple anymore. I am a failure."

Are you one who goes back like Peter and fishes out memories from the past? Maybe you listen to demons who tell you that you are a failure and that there is no hope. And the more you think about it, the more you end up agreeing with those thoughts: "I am too much of a sinner," you say. "I don't know if I can make it."

Perhaps you just don't know how to get back up again after failure. Maybe you don't feel that you can trust yourself anymore. Maybe you can't imagine that people will believe in you again.

We may not be able to trust ourselves, but we can trust God. Read the words of Saint John Chrysostom, who walked closely with God in the early days of the Church: "God is called a God of consolation, a God of mercy, because he is constantly working to encourage and console those who are distressed and afflicted even if they have sinned ten thousand times."[4]

God believes in you. Peter's life did not end in destruction and despair. God is greater than all your failures too.

Physical Exhaustion

Physical weariness and health problems can cause discouragement too. Our bodies get tired, hungry and sick, and it seems we are too discouraged to go on. Elijah experienced this. He was so exhausted that an angel had to tell him, "Get up and eat" (1 Kings 19:5).

It happens to me too. Sometimes I don't want to see anyone. I think about how overwhelming the task is, and by that alone, I feel worn out.

Self-Sufficiency

Another reason for discouragement is pride and an unbroken spirit. One of the surest ways for discouragement to find its way into our lives is when we are unwilling to admit that we can't accomplish everything in our own strength. When we resist God's grace and insist that we are sufficient, we exhaust ourselves and get nowhere.

If there ever was a man who could have easily relied on his own strength, on his powerful heritage and education, it was the Apostle Paul. Added to that was the amazing experience of being taken into the heavens and shown incredible things. This was so wonderful that Paul wasn't given permission to say anything about the revelations he had seen (see 2 Corinthians 12:1–4).

Yet it was Paul who pleaded with the Lord three times that his "thorn in the flesh" might be removed. It sounds like he was discouraged by his circumstances, and his expectations were unmet. But God replied to his pleas, "My grace is sufficient for you, for My strength is made perfect in weakness" (2 Corinthians 12:9, NKJV).

When we are depending on ourselves, God will often use discouraging circumstances to show us our need for Him. Godly Bible teacher Zac Poonen tells us,

> When God orders your circumstances in such a way that you are disappointed on every side, that shouldn't discourage you. It is just God weaning you away from the arm of the flesh so that you might learn to live by faith in Him.[5]

The psalmist answers his own question in Psalm 42:5 with, "Hope in God, for I shall again praise Him for the help of His presence" (Psalm 42:5b, NASB). And that trust is the beginning of our way to victory.

CHAPTER THREE

The Way to Victory

———•••———

If we are to find the way to victory, we must understand the spiritual dimension of discouragement. There are powers of darkness, the principalities in high places at work in discouragement. Ephesians 6:12 says, "For our struggle is not against flesh and blood, but against the rulers, against the authorities, against the powers of this dark world and against the spiritual forces of evil in the heavenly realms." We should not be caught unaware of Satan's schemes (see 2 Corinthians 2:11). Demons use thoughts and imaginations to pull us down.

Although our discouragement may at times seem hopeless, there is victory in this battle! We are able to stand firm in the full armor of God.

Choosing to Fight

Once we recognize the source of discouragement, we have to make a choice. We have to choose to say, "I will *not* continue living in the realm of discouragement and despair." It is a choice we must make of our own volition. We must decide with our own free will to fight these schemes of the Enemy.

So what does that look like in real life? When confronted with the forces of darkness, how do we choose freedom? How do we cast down negative thoughts?

In 2 Corinthians 10:4–5, Paul says:

> The weapons we fight with are not the weapons of the world. On the contrary, they have divine power to demolish strongholds. We demolish arguments and every pretension that sets itself up against the knowledge of God, and we take captive every thought to make it obedient to Christ.

So that is our responsibility. It is not an impossible task because we remember that we are told, "No weapon forged against you will prevail" (Isaiah 54:17). We can cast down these negative thoughts in the name of Jesus. We can destroy these thoughts of despair that cause damage to our inner life. We can stand strong on the foundation of Christ and His Word and fight discouragement. He tells us we will win. You will be victorious.

Some years ago, I had a phone call from a mother with four children. She told me, "I am on the verge of suicide." And she went on to explain, "When I finished college, I thought I would do something wonderful with my life. Someone even suggested I could be a movie star. Someone else said I could write poems and stories. But now I'm at the point where I have to force myself to get out of bed. I have lost all motivation. I live with constant criticism from my husband. Life is worthless."

I told this woman, "The only way you can overcome your situation is to stop focusing on what your husband is doing or not doing for you. You must deal with *your* attitude, *your* response to the situation. Use the weapons God has given you."

She asked me, "But how do I do that? I pray. I fast. What else can I do?" Then she started crying.

I said, "Find a quiet place where you are alone. Then open your mouth and say, 'In Jesus' name, I stand against this demonic attack. I am worth something to God, and I am made in His image. I am not going to let the devil destroy me. I belong to Jesus. I am His child.'" Then I instructed her to repeat that five times a day for the next 21 days.

A few months later, I received another phone call from her. She said, "I did exactly what you told me to do. My husband's attitude toward me hasn't changed. The condition of my home hasn't changed. But I am completely free. I can't believe it. I am no longer the same person. I am totally transformed."

Spiritual realities can never become authentic and tangible unless we choose to engage in battle. Martyn Lloyd-Jones encourages us to take action against the Enemy:

> When Satan, your adversary, comes and tries to drive you to the depth of despair and dejection . . . turn upon him and say, "I have an advocate with the Father, Jesus Christ the righteous. . . . I am accepted by God, the fellowship is restored, and I continue upon my way."[1]

But unless you choose to fight and stand in truth, your battle won't be won. If you sit by passively and say, "God will help me," you will stay emotionally sick and mentally tormented. You have to respond and stand firm. You must choose not to accept despair.

Steps to Take in Battling Discouragement

Once we have chosen to fight discouragement, what are the next steps to take?

First, to overcome despair we have to *see beyond the present problem*. Hebrews 12:2 says that Christ, "for the joy set before him endured the cross." What did He see? Was it the pain, the torture, the cross that He saw? No, He saw beyond all that to eternity, to a Bride by His side, purchased by His own blood for the pleasure of His Father.

In your disappointments, strive to see beyond them to God's grace. The problems you face right now are helping you become the man or woman God desires you to be. You are being transformed into the image of His Son.

Remember Joseph? He was a real-life, flesh-and-blood young man, not at all unlike you or me. This righteous, godly individual was sold as a slave into Egypt by his brothers and then put in prison for a wrong he had not done. He had to face 13 long years of discouragement there, forgotten and forsaken.

But through it all, Joseph saw something beyond his imprisonment and struggles; something beyond his torment kept him hoping. He knew God had a plan and a reason for it all. A day was going to come when his dream would come to pass.

Do you have a dream? What is it? Hope in Christ. Dream the promises of God:

- "The last will be first, and the first will be last" (Matthew 20:16).

- "He has done everything well" (Mark 7:37).

- "I am with you always, to the very end of the age" (Matthew 28:20).

- Remember, there waits for you a "city which has foundations, whose builder and maker is God" (Hebrews 11:10, NKJV).

This journey will not be very long. This earthly existence is not the end of our lives. We are faced with a battle, but victory awaits us. God is sovereign, and Romans 8:28 is true: "And we know that in all things God works for the good of those who love him, who have been called according to his purpose."

God uses the present crisis, the misunderstandings, the pain and the discouraging circumstances to mold us in preparation for eternal life in heaven.

Second, to fight discouragement, we must *remember that it is our privilege to suffer for Christ*. Meditate on Him. In your suffering, "consider him who endured such opposition from sinful men, so that you will not grow weary and lose heart" (Hebrews 12:3).

In the early days of the ministry, when faced with misunderstanding, pain, accusations and rejection, I would cry out to the Lord and say, "Why did this happen to me? Why must I suffer like this? Why?"

Then one day I was meditating on the words that Paul wrote to the church in Philippi—words he wrote while sitting chained in a prison for the sake of Christ: "I want to know Christ . . . and the fellowship of sharing in his sufferings" (Philippians 3:10).

The Lord helped me understand the meaning of "not wasting my sorrows." I began to see how my suffering could become meaningful if I allowed the cross to enter into my pain. Then I was able to say, "Lord, now I know how You suffered when You were mistreated and rejected. Now I know how lonely You felt . . . now I finally understand what You went through."

For three days after the children of Israel were miraculously freed from Egypt, they had nothing to drink. When they finally came upon some water in Marah, they could not drink it because it was so bitter.

But even the bitterest of waters turned into sweet water when a piece of wood was placed in it (see Exodus 15:22–25). In the same way, allowing the cross to enter into our suffering can turn it into sweet fellowship with our Lord.

Third, in our fight against discouragement, we must *take the time to rest in silence, waiting upon God and putting our hope in the Lord.* Just be silent and take time to meditate. Isaiah 40:30–31 says,

> Even youths grow tired and weary, and young men stumble and fall; but those who hope in the Lord will renew their strength. They will soar on wings like eagles; they will run and not grow weary, they will walk and not be faint.

Through quieting ourselves, we are able to focus on God alone. He is the only One bigger than our discouragement.

Fourth, *remember that one of the most powerful elements in the battle against discouragement is words.* The power to give life or to crush life is in the tongue (see Proverbs 18:21). God spoke and the world came into existence out of nothing. We are created in the image of God, so we are created to use words like He does. Yet so often we use words to destroy, discourage, put down and judge.

The words that we speak and confess with our mouth can be life or death. Words spoken to us, words that we speak to others and words that we say to ourselves are all powerful.

When you say to yourself, "I'm not able. This is too hard. I'm going to be sick. I'm going to die," you are only sowing to the wind and reaping the whirlwind.

When the children of Israel were spying out the Promised Land, they reported on the dangers they saw and said, "If only we had died in Egypt! Or in this desert!" (Numbers 14:2). God took these words that they spoke in complaining and essentially said, "So shall it be" (see Numbers 14:26–29). Nothing good can come of speaking negatively.

Just as damaging are the negative words that are spoken to us. I have begun a certain practice as a remedy for these. When somebody tells me something that is negative or discouraging, I simply say to myself, "In the name of Jesus, I reject this. I refuse to receive these words that are spoken to me." By fighting those negative words with words of life, I am no longer affected by them. It's amazing!

Talk to the devil if you need to. I promise you, it works! But do it in Jesus' name. Don't go in your name or anyone else's. Unless you stand in the power of Jesus' name, the devil will not listen to you.

God has not called us to be influenced by untrue things said about us, but instead to keep from the trappings of this world. Don't fall into a pattern of negative thinking, "but be transformed by the renewing of your mind" (Romans 12:2).

It is up to you how you respond to negative words. So be firm! Don't be dragged down by them. Remember Christ's words to you and stand on those instead:

- "Never will I leave you; never will I forsake you" (Hebrews 13:5).

- "The Word became flesh and made his dwelling among us" (John 1:14).

- "I can do everything through him who gives me strength" (Philippians 4:13).

Claim these promises when you face difficulties. Hold up what the Bible says and speak these words of truth into your life and the lives of others.

Ephesians 6:17 says, "Take the helmet of salvation and the sword of the Spirit, which is the word of God." Fight with this weapon, remembering promises like, "I am the Lord, who heals you" (Exodus 15:26). Hang on to that. Believe it. In every situation, believe. Be like Moses and see Him who is invisible (see Hebrews 11:27).

Fifth, *pray with someone.* Hebrews 10:25 says, "Let us not give up meeting together, as some are in the habit of doing, but let us encourage one another—and all the more as you see the Day approaching."

Encourage one another! Seek out times to share and pray with a friend. Let the Body of Christ minister to you in your problems. Remember this promise: "For where two or three come together in my name, there am I with them" (Matthew 18:20).

Sixth, *realize that God's love for you has nothing to do with your holiness, your purity, how well you did or how badly you sinned.* God cannot change. He is love. Just like the sun always gives out light, God always gives out love no matter what you have done. It is only the devil who whispers to you and says, "Because of your mistakes, God doesn't love you."

God's truth is quite different than the devil's lies, says Zac Poonen: "Find your security in the fact that God loves you as He loved Jesus."[2] And Paul tells us in Romans 5:8, "But God demonstrates his own love for us in this: While we were still sinners, Christ died for us." Allow God to keep that promise alive in you.

The devil must have whispered to Peter, "You failed Him in the garden when you slept. You failed Him by denying Him three times before the rooster crowed. You failed Him by returning to your fishing boat and taking the others with you."

But Jesus didn't bring up any of these failures. Instead, He asked Peter, "Do you love Me?" And when Peter said, "Yes," then Jesus essentially said, "I know that you love Me even with all your struggles and difficulties. That is good enough for Me. Peter, feed My sheep" (see John 21). It is important that we comprehend His love and His grace, grace that is greater than all our sin.

Seventh, *don't be a loner.* Don't miss an opportunity to be with brothers and sisters in the Lord. You are loved by God, and He shows His love to you through others. Be open to receive it.

Never think that you are alone. Find someone to share your struggles with and to pray with. Recall the love and affection you have experienced in the past from others.

Eighth, *do it all for Jesus.* When you feel alone, when nobody understands you, don't give up. Even though you can't see what God is doing, you have no reason to quit. Keep doing the right thing, not for recognition or praise from others or so you can feel good about yourself. Do everything for Him.

I heard a story once about a band of minstrels performing many years ago in Europe. It was wintertime, and the snow kept falling. Fewer and fewer people came to watch their performances. One day, one of the members of the troupe said, "Why bother performing? No one comes to watch us. Let's close up and go home."

But an older member stood up and said, "No, we must keep to our purpose. It doesn't matter if only one or two come. Let's perform better than ever before."

That night they gathered their courage and put on their best show yet. Very few people showed up to watch. However, after the show, one of the troupe members was handed a note.

"I thoroughly enjoyed your performance. Excellent job. I loved it." The note was signed, "Your king." Nobody knew until that moment that the king had been there, but he had been watching.[3]

Maybe it doesn't seem like anyone ever watches or appreciates you. Maybe no one on this earth understands you. But your King is always watching you. Do it all for Him.

CHAPTER FOUR

Encouragement in Christ

———•••———

Christ often visited the home of two sisters, Mary and Martha, who both cared deeply for Jesus and His disciples. The way Martha expressed her love and concern was to cook a fine meal. But in the middle of these preparations, she came to Christ and said, "Lord, don't you care that my sister has left me to do the work by myself? Tell her to help me!" (Luke 10:40).

In other words, she said, "Lord, this is not fair. Why do You allow Mary to sit here, so relaxed and happy, while I am killing myself back in this hot, stuffy kitchen? This just isn't right!"

Think about Martha's side of the story. Could it be that she felt discouraged because she was not appreciated? Sometimes, when I think about this story, I want to read next that Christ came to the kitchen door and said, "Martha, I know how hard you are working for us. Thank you so much!"

But I know this was not the way that Jesus thought. I don't think like He does, but perhaps my carnal nature reveals what Martha was thinking in this instance. We can begin to feel what she might have been feeling. We would have liked for Jesus to have encouraged her in her work.

But instead Jesus replied, "Martha, Martha . . . you are worried and upset about many things, but only one thing is needed. Mary has chosen what is better, and it will not be taken away from her" (Luke 10:41–42).

Having the Right Priority

Why couldn't Jesus encourage Martha in the work that she was doing? Maybe more hard work wasn't the priority He wanted her to have. We humans have a hang-up; we need to feel appreciated in what we do. But Jesus chose not to meet this need in Martha be-cause it would have led her along a path away from intimacy with Him.

Blessed is the man or woman who encour-ages anyone to look to Christ alone. Saint John Chrysostom says,

> Encourage one another to remain standing just as you have been standing. If anyone wavers from the ranks, take care to hold him back. In this way you will receive a double reward, for your own zeal and for the concern you show for your brothers.[1]

Encourage others to seek God. Do not encourage them to blindly continue down the same path; rather, encourage them to seek Christ and serve Him in joyful and restful obedience.

Sometimes no one will notice how faithfully we serve. You and I are human beings, and in this fragile life of ours, there are times when deep down we long for someone to know and appreciate what we do. We want someone to recognize us. Often we want this because we are consumed with ourselves.

It is precisely at these moments that we must be reminded to look to Christ. It is then that our brothers and sisters may be clear examples of Christ to us and guide us to Him. The following poem I wrote expresses this thought:

You Be My Jesus

The night is darker than the darkest night
not a star in the sky.
Cruel storm howls in distance
　　　creating piercing silence.
Non-stop downpour.
It seems this night is forever.

My lamp is empty
　　　only left the smoking wick
　　　　　hurting my eyes
forcing me to shut them in the dark.

Is there anyone who cares
　　　to understand
to say a kind word
　　　to lend a helping hand?
Yes, I know Jesus cares
Jesus understands.

But I don't see Him
　　　can't touch Him
　　　　　Where is He?

Till I find Him
Please stay with me
Please take my hand.

It is so dark.
YOU BE MY JESUS
I am all alone.
　　　Alone.[2]

It's not often that we express these feelings so plainly or that someone comes to us and tells us these things, but these words are true for all of us at one time or another. It is our responsibility to be Christ to others and encourage them to look to Him to sustain their life.

He Is Sufficient

So why didn't Jesus confirm Martha's work? As much as He may have wanted to, He couldn't, because He was using this disappointment to purify Martha from needs that were not heavenly.

Many times He deals similarly with us. Saint Augustine in his Confessions recalls the purpose of the hard times of his youth: to turn away from his immoral actions and follow Christ. He says to God, "You were ever present to me, . . . sprinkling very bitter disappointments over all my unlawful pleasures so that I might seek a pleasure free from all disappointment."[3]

The writings of Dr. E. Stanley Jones have had a huge impact on my life. He was a devout follower of Christ and one of the greatest missionary statesmen of the 20th century, impacting millions for Christ.

I have had the privilege of listening to some of his teachings on tape. Once I remember him talking about a discovery he had made, a secret that worked to free him from worry, care and discouragement.

Early in his work, he was carrying all the burdens himself, and as a result of that strain, he had two nervous breakdowns. In despair one night during his travels, he found himself at a church service in Lucknow, India.

While they were praying, the Lord spoke to him and said, "Look, Stanley, are you ready to turn your life over to Me, or do you want to hang on to it and ruin it? If you give it to Me, I will take care of you and give you the energy and strength. You will not be destroyed by depression and discouragement."

At that very moment, Dr. Jones surrendered his life to the Lord and everything with it. He testifies that his life was changed forever.

We are raised with a philosophy of social conditioning that makes us believe turning our life over to an unseen Savior looks irrational and stupid. We are taught that only a simple, weak-willed person would consider that Christ might be the answer to all of our life's choices and the turmoil that we face.

The truth is this: The Lord Jesus Christ is the answer to all that we face in life, including disappointment and discouragement.

David dealt with his need for encouragement by going to God. When he faced the tremendous loneliness and sorrow of being abandoned by even his closest friends, the Scriptures tell us that "David encouraged himself in the Lord his God" (1 Samuel 30:6, KJV).

Paul also encouraged the Thessalonians to be encouraged in Christ. Second Thessalonians 2:16–17 says, "May our Lord Jesus Christ himself and God our Father, who loved us and by his grace gave us eternal encouragement and good hope, encourage your hearts and strengthen you in every good deed and word."

So when you are faced with disappointments and when all around you seems hopeless, do not give up or try to solve the problem yourself. Satan tries to use these disappointments to discourage you and bring you down, but God can use them for a better purpose.

Go to Christ instead. He is able to lead you out of your discouragement. And if you focus on Him, He will use times of trials in your life to bring you closer to Him. You need only to look to Him. He is willing. *Make your choice.*

Prayer

Lord, thank You for Your promise that in times of trouble, You would meet every need. Some of us need encouragement. We want affirmation, but we don't have it. Lord, be our Encourager.

Throughout Scripture, Your people went through difficult times. You never left them, not in the deepest, darkest valleys. So this day, Lord, we tell You, we trust You. We will get through this. We will come to the other side. We will be established in You and will not be overtaken by our circumstances, for You reign in us. And You are able.

Thank You for the reminder that You never forsake us. Thank You for blessing us with brothers and sisters to walk alongside us in this journey. Thank You that we are Your sons and daughters. You are our joy, our peace and our strength. Thank You for hope for today.

Give us the ability to be encouragers to others and to be a source of strength. Enable us to withstand discouragement and to choose the way of victory. Help us to stay close to You and remain strong in this battle. We trust You, and we thank You, Lord. In Jesus' name, Amen.

If this booklet has been a blessing to you,
I would really like to hear from you.
You may write to:

Gospel for Asia

1800 Golden Trail Court

Carrollton, TX 75010

Or send an email to kp@gfa.org.

Notes

—••—

Chapter 1

[1] Definition taken from http://www.webster-dictionary.net/definition/discouragement.

[2] Martyn Lloyd-Jones, *Life in Christ: Studies in 1 John* (Wheaton, IL: Crossway Books, 2002), p. 338.

Chapter 2

[1] Stephen R. Covey, *The Seven Habits of Highly Effective People* (New York, NY: Fireside, 1989), p. 28.

[2] A.W. Tozer, *TOZER: Fellowship of the Burning Heart*, ed., *James L. Snyder* (Alachua, FL: Bridge-Logos, 2006), p. 157.

[3] Adapted from Michael L. Brown, *How Saved Are We?* (Shippensburg, PA: Destiny Image Publishers, 1990), pp. 96–99.

[4] Saint John Chrysostom, *On the Incomprehensible Nature of God*, trans., Paul W. Harkins (Washington, DC: The Catholic University of America Press, Inc., 1984), p. 163.

[5] Zac Poonen, *"Secrets of Victory"* (1982).

Chapter 3

[1] Lloyd-Jones, *Life in Christ: Studies in 1 John*, p. 179.

[2] Poonen, *"Secrets of Victory."*

[3] Adapted from *God's Little Devotional Journal for Women* (Colorado Springs, CO: Honor Books, 2000), p. 87.

Chapter 4

[1] Chrysostom, *On the Incomprehensible Nature of God, p. 114.*

[2] K.P. Yohannan, *"You Be My Jesus."*

[3] Saint Augustine, *The Confessions, trans., Maria Boulding (New York, NY: Vintage Books, 1997), p. 26.*

Booklets by K.P. Yohannan

A Life of Balance
Remember learning how to ride a bike? It was all a matter of balance. The same is true for our lives. Learn how to develop that balance, which will keep your life and ministry healthy and honoring God. (80 pages)

Dependence upon the Lord
Don't build in vain. Learn how to daily depend upon the Lord—whether in the impossible or the possible—and see your life bear lasting fruit. (48 pages)

Discouragement: Reasons and Answers
Ready to defeat discouragement and move on? It can be done! Discover the reasons for discouragement, and find hope and strength for an overcoming life. (56 pages)

Journey with Jesus
Take this invitation to walk the roads of life intimately with the Lord Jesus. Stand with the disciples and learn from Jesus' example of love, humility, power and surrender. (56 pages)

Learning to Pray
Whether you realize it or not, your prayers change things. Be hindered no longer as K.P. Yohannan shares how you can grow in your daily prayer life. See for yourself how God still does the impossible through prayer. (64 pages)

Living by Faith, Not by Sight
The promises of God are still true today: *"Anything is possible to him who believes!"* This balanced teaching will remind you of the power of God and encourage you to step out in childlike faith. (56 pages)

Principles in Maintaining a Godly Organization
Remember the "good old days" in your ministry? This booklet provides a biblical basis for maintaining that vibrancy and commitment that accompany any new move of God. (48 pages)

Seeing Him
Do you often live just day-to-day, going through the routine of life? We so easily lose sight of Him who is our everything. Through this booklet, let the Lord Jesus restore your heart and eyes to see Him again. (48 pages)

Stay Encouraged
How are you doing? Discouragement can sneak in quickly and subtly, through even the smallest things. Learn how to stay encouraged in every season of life, no matter what the circumstances may be. (56 pages)

That They All May Be One
In this booklet, K.P. Yohannan opens up his heart and shares from past struggles and real-life examples on how to maintain unity with those in our lives. A must read! (56 pages)

The Beauty of Christ through Brokenness
We were made in the image of Christ that we may reflect all that He is to the hurting world around us. Rise above the things that hinder you from doing this, and see how your life can display His beauty, power and love. (72 pages)

The Lord's Work Done in the Lord's Way
Tired? Burned out? Weary? The Lord's work done in His way will never destroy you. Learn what it means to minister unto Him and keep the holy love for Him burning strong even in the midst of intense ministry. A must-read for every believer! (72 pages)

The Way of True Blessing
What does God value most? Find out in this booklet as K.P. Yohannan reveals truths from the life of Abraham, an ordinary man who became the friend of God. (56 pages)

When We Have Failed—What Next?
The best is yet to come. Do you find that hard to believe? If failure has clouded your vision to see God's redemptive power, this booklet is for you. God's ability to work out His best plan for your life remains. Believe it. (88 pages)

Order booklets through:
Gospel for Asia, 1800 Golden Trail Court, Carrollton, TX 75010
Toll free: 1-800-WIN-ASIA
Online: www.gfa.org

REVOLUTION
IN WORLD MISSIONS

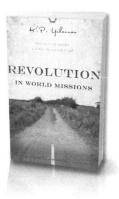

Step into the story of missionary statesman K.P. Yohannan and experience the world through his eyes. You will hang on every word—from the villages of India to the shores of Europe and North America. Watch out: His passion is contagious! (240 pages)

When We Have Failed — What Next?

The best *is* yet to come. Do you find that hard to believe? If failure has clouded your vision to see God's redemptive power, this booklet is for you. God's ability to work out His best plan for your life remains. Believe it. (88 pages)